MW01514578

PARTICIPANT'S GUIDE

GODONOMIC$
What the **ALMIGHTY** says about the almighty dollar.

SMALL GROUP CURRICULUM

www.godonomics.com

Published by God Quest, INC. Pensacola, FL

© 2010

Author **Chad Hovind**

Designer Kaylee Kelso

Copyright © God Quest, INC.

No part of this book may be reproduced or transmitted in any form or by any means, electronic or mechanical, including photocopying and recording, or by any information storage or retrieval system, except as may be expressly permitted in writing by the publishers. Requests for permission should be addressed in writing to God Quest;

P.O. Box 37338, Pensacola, FL 32526.

ISBN 978-1-58468-502-9

Item # 44110PG

Subject heading: GODONOMICS: WHAT THE ALMIGHTY SAYS ABOUT THE ALMIGHTY DOLLAR / PARTICIPANT'S GUIDE

This book is the Participant's Guide for the small group curriculum course *Godonomics*, an informational DVD series on Biblical Economics.

Scripture taken from the New King James Version.

Copyright © 1982 by Thomas Nelson, Inc.

Used by permission. All rights reserved.

To order additional copies of this resource:

Phone/Customer Service 1-877-479-3466 (Toll free USA only)

1-850-479 -3466; Order Online at *www.godonomics.com*; or Visit

The Creation Store

5800 North "W." St, Suite 9

Pensacola, FL 32505.

Printed in the United States of America

Chad Hovind is Senior Pastor of Horizon Community Church in Cincinnati, Ohio. Graduating from Moody Bible Institute in Chicago, Illinois, in 1995, he majored in pastoral ministry and communication. His love for ministry and creativity can be seen in many forms: leading teams, expository teaching, acting, and video production. Prior to his pastorate at Horizon, Chad served as pastor at two high-impact churches in Georgia: Cumberland Community Church and New Community Church. In 2009, Chad received his M.A. in Ministry from Moody Bible Institute. He loves volleyball, movies, and hanging out with his wife, Beth, and their three children.

CHAD HOVIND

"Simple enough to teach kids—researched enough for the Wall Street Journal. *Godonomics* is a must-see if you care about your country."

Bob McEwen
Former US Congressman

"Nobody has done a better job of applying Biblical principles to economics. If you believe in the Bible and are concerned about the economy, you've got to see this."

Phil Heimlich
Hamilton County Commissioner of Cincinnati, Ohio

CONTENTS

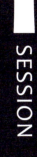

ADAM SMITH

"WHAT WOULD GOD SAY TO ADAM SMITH?"

"The natural effort of every individual to better his own condition...is so **powerful** a principle, *that it is alone capable of carrying on the society to* **wealth** *and* **prosperity...**surmounting **a hundred obstructions** with which the *folly of human laws* **too often** encumbers its operations. The *drive for greater government regulation* is the drive toward **INCREASED poverty**, **unemployment**, and the loss of **liberty**."

— Adam Smith

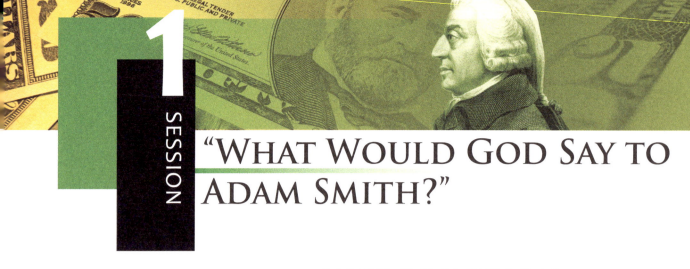

"WHAT WOULD GOD SAY TO ADAM SMITH?"

INTRODUCTION

In this first session of *Godonomics*, you will learn the basics of Capitalism, Profit, and Work. You'll discover that the father of modern capitalism was a Christian named Adam Smith who showed how God's principles of liberty, prosperity, and generosity could change an individual, a family, and even a national economy—and it sure did! As his principles were applied, a wave of prosperity washed across Europe and spilled into America in the 1800's. We'll see that profit truly is a gift from God when it is focused on meeting others' needs rather than personal greed.

Many employers today are finding that Generation Y lacks the proper business skills to launch from college into the work force. Session 1 covers some basics of running a business and how to pay employees and set up pay scales in your company in a way that pays people fairly, not equally.

Matthew 25:26-28
26 But his lord answered and said to him, 'You wicked and lazy servant, you knew that I reap where I have not sown, and gather where I have not scattered seed. 27 So you ought to have deposited my money with the bankers, and at my coming I would have received back my own with interest. 28 Therefore take the talent from him, and give it to him who has ten talents.

In addition, this session gives us an example of how to teach our kids strong work ethic and eliminate the entitlement attitude that keeps our kids and our society from experiencing their full potential. If you've ever felt the guilt of a family member who is mooching off you, this chapter helps you understand that there are times to help those in need and times not to enable others' bad behavior.

Proverbs 31 sums up how a good economy works: The Proverbs 31 woman begins by finding a vineyard that PRODUCES. She PROFITS from it. Then from her SAVINGS, she INVESTS in another vineyard allowing her to GIVE to the poor and needy, hire more workers, and SPEND. This Bible passage demonstrates the power of the free market—affirming property rights, incentive, and freedom.

STUDY GUIDE

$hare in Prayer

$ee the Godly Perspective

Is profit a good thing or a bad thing? Since God offered his wisdom on so many subjects, doesn't it make sense that He'd offer wisdom on principles of economics, too? Let's look at our own finances from God's perspective. Is God in control of them? On a national scale, in the time it will have taken you to read this sentence, the United States national debt will have increased by about $200,000. Surely, run-away debt is not a result of godly principles. How different would things be if we instituted *Godonomics* at every level of society?

$earch For Truth

In this first session, notice the failure of socialism's early experiment in America's history. Note how a centralized approach to economics is both inefficient and unscriptural. Learn to what source Adam Smith turned for direction when socialism failed.

2 Thessalonians 3: 7-9

[7] For you yourselves know how you ought to follow us, for we were not disorderly among you; [8] nor did we eat anyone's bread free of charge, but worked with labor and toil night and day, that we might not be a burden to any of you, [9] not because we do not have authority, but to make ourselves an example of how you should follow us.

Throughout history, Christ's followers have succeeded in many areas where others have failed, including financial endeavors, simply by following God's Word. Watch for God's foundational sequence laid out in this first session of Production, Profit, and Savings. This approach to capitalism stands in stark contrast to the consumer-based approach commonly accepted today. *Godonomics* is all about following God's order in finances which leads to greater ability and freedom to serve God, to provide for ourselves, and to bless others. A reoccurring theme throughout our study will be that God desperately wants us to experience liberty, prosperity, and generosity. Let's delve into the first principles of *GODONOMICS*---the Gift of Work, and the Gift of Profit!

$tart the DVD $ession and $pecify the Worksheet Answers

(32 minutes)

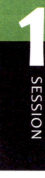

WORKSHEET

When he landed in America, Governor_____tried an
(1)
experiment in socialism that ended in disaster.

Three Components of Capitalism are:_____,
(2)
_____,(or Liberty) and _____.
(3)   (4)

In 1776, Adam Smith, the Father of Modern Capitalism, wrote a book
entitled _____which included Godly principles of
(5)
capitalism that eventually influenced the structure of the U.S. economy.
God wants us to experience_____, _____, and
(6)   (7)
_____.
(8)

I. The Gift of _____.
(9)

- Work is from God: Genesis 2:15

- Work for God: Colossians 3:23-24

- Work for Self-Sufficiency to bear your own load: Galatians 6:4-5

- Work is mandated in 2 Thessalonians 3:7-12, affirming the components of capitalism.

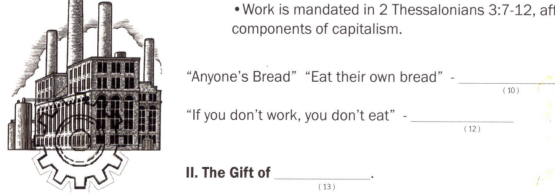

"Anyone's Bread" "Eat their own bread" - _____ _____
(10)   (11)

"If you don't work, you don't eat" - _____
(12)

II. The Gift of _____.
(13)

WORKSHEET

1

SESSION

The $ix $tages of *Godonomics*

G_____
(14)

P_____
(15)

P_____
(16)

S_____
(17)

I_____
(18)

S_____
(19)

Proverbs 31

      [16]She **considers** a field and buys it; from **her profits** she plants a vineyard... [18]She perceives that her merchandise is good, and her lamp does not go out by night... [27]And **does not eat the bread of idleness**. [20]She extends her hand to **the poor**, yes, she reaches out her **hands to the needy**. [31]Give her of the **fruit of her hands**.

Treat and pay people _____, not _____.
                             (20)   (21)

"The drive for greater government regulation is a drive toward increased_____, _____, and the loss of
                         (22)   (23)
_____."
(24)
Capitalism does not eliminate _____, but it neutralizes it.
                                    (25)

God the father loved us so much, that He sent His son, Jesus Christ, to earth to die for us. As a believer in Jesus Christ, we are _____
                                                          (26)
_____ with Him to all the riches of a loving Heavenly Father!
(27)
(Romans 8:17 "And if children, then heirs; heirs of God, and joint-heirs with Christ..."

ADDITIONAL READING:

How the Scots Invented the Modern World
By Arthur Herman

Victory of Reason
By Rodney Stark

SESSION 1

WORKSHEET SCORE KEY

1) William Bradford

2) Property Rights

3) Freedom

4) Incentive

5) The Wealth of the Nations

6) liberty

7) prosperity

8) generosity

9) Work

10) Property

11) Rights

12) Incentive

13) Profit

14) Giving

15) Producing

16) Profitting

17) Saving

18) Investing

19) Spending

20) fairly

21) equally

22) poverty

23) unemployment

24) liberty

25) greed

26) joint

27) heirs

Settle the Discussion Questions

1. What are three primary elements of *Godonomics* — style capitalism, and how might each of them facilitate a more prosperous and Christian lifestyle? _____

   _____

   _____

   _____

   _____

2. Socialism seeks to control and intervene in the economy to treat people equally, but how might laissez-faire — free market capitalism — be a better system, and in what way might a government-run economy be contrary to Scripture? _____

   _____

   _____

   _____

   _____

   _____

3. What is *Godonomics*? What are the steps an individual should follow concerning their finances according to this model?

   _____

   _____

   _____

   _____

Study the Summary Statements

When we follow God's rules and model for economics, we will work as unto the Lord, yielding a profit. In turn, we will be able to give and to invest. In Proverbs 13:22, the Bible tells us, "A good man leaveth an inheritance to his children's children." In reality, this is no magic potion. *Godonomics* is not a get-rich-quick scheme. It is a set of godly principles in which one is not enslaved to debt. Income is real profit, something more than just a means to make the monthly payments. When *Godonomics* is applied on a national scale, the national economy, too, is as prosperous as the laborers and investors are willing to labor to produce. Protecting property rights and seeking limited government allows the incentives of honest profits to reward those who take the initiative.

> 2 Thessalonians 3: 10-12
>
> [10] For even when we were with you, we commanded you this: If anyone will not work, neither shall he eat. [11] For we hear that there are some who walk among you in a disorderly manner, not working at all, but are busybodies. [12] Now those who are such we command and exhort through our Lord Jesus Christ that they work in quietness and eat their own bread.

Instilling these principles of investing, saving, and working in our children is also important. We need to train our children to seek fair reward for their labors—not equal benefits.

Throughout history, God has blessed individuals and nations who worked hard for their profit and honored Him with their increase. We can be assured that everyone has their own work interest at heart. However, when yielded to God, our labor can lead to prosperity and greater generosity promoting both self sufficiency and the ability to give and meet the needs of society as the Lord leads. These principles form the bedrock of *Godonomics*.

$how $upport

Go around your group, having someone read each of the following sentences and the verse that goes with it. After you've read all eight, discuss the following questions. As a whole, how would society be better if we followed God's principles of work? Which of the Employee/Employer commandments stand out to you?

What the Bible says to an Employer:
1. Serve, not "use," my employees by paying them fairly.
   (Matthew 20:26)

2. Hold my employees accountable.
   (Matthew 16:27)

3. Pay my employees fairly and promptly.
   (Malachi 3:5; Deuteronomy 24:14-15)

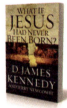

4. Work like God is your boss.
   (Colossians 3:23-24)

ADDITIONAL READING:

What If Jesus Had Never Been Born?

By Dr. D. James Kennedy

What the Bible says to an Employee:
1. Work hard and diligently.
   (Ecclesiastes 9:10)

2. Work honestly by not cheating your boss.
   (Daniel 6:4)

3. Don't be lazy.
   (2 Thessalonians 3:10)

4. Work like God is your boss.
   (Colossians 3:23-24)

Scripture to Savor

2 Thessalonians 3:8-10

       [8] nor did we eat anyone's bread **free of charge**, but **worked with labor and toil night and day**, that we might **not be a burden** to any of you, [9] not because we do not have authority, but **to make ourselves an example of how you should follow us**. [10] For even when we were with you, we commanded you this: If anyone **will not work, neither shall he eat**.

"So . . . What *Would* God Say to Adam Smith?"

WHO'S YOUR BARBER?
WORK, PROPERTY RIGHTS, AND INCENTIVES
ARE BLESSINGS FROM ME.
~ GOD

JOHN KEYNES

"What Would God Say to John Keynes?"

"A government **BIG** *enough to* give everything you want**, is BIG ENOUGH** to take away everything you have."

— Thomas Jefferson

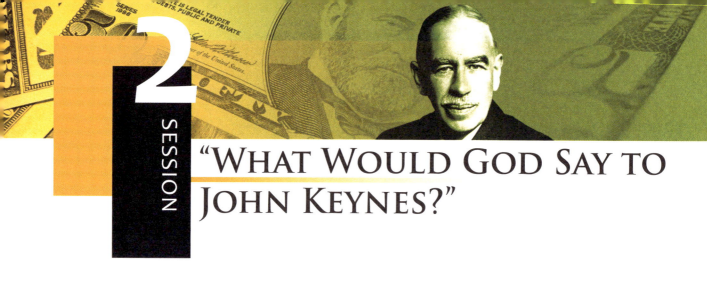

"WHAT WOULD GOD SAY TO JOHN KEYNES?"

INTRODUCTION

In our second session, "What Would God Say to John Keynes?" we'll discover how Keynesian Economics and *Godonomics* are polar opposites! Even if you have never heard of John Keynes, you witness daily how his ideas are today's blueprint for the concept of money management as well as the economic policies of most governments. Individuals, marriages, and nations are all under severe stress from debt caused by spending more than we have and paying ever increasing interest on credit. Our children are losing their liberty as our national debt skyrockets into the trillions of dollars. Proverbs tells us to leave an inheritance to our children's children, not a bill from our gluttonous spending.

Delve into Session Two of *Godonomics* where we'll learn two important slogans: "Spend your way to slavery, not prosperity!" and "Act your own wage!"

Matthew 25:24–29

24 Then he who had received the one talent came and said, 'Lord, I knew you to be a hard man, reaping where you have not sown, and gathering where you have not scattered seed. 25 And I was afraid, and went and hid your talent in the ground. Look, there you have what is yours.' 26 But his lord answered and said to him, 'You wicked and lazy servant, you knew that I reap where I have not sown, and gather where I have not scattered seed. 27 So you ought to have deposited my money with the bankers, and at my coming I would have received back my own with interest. 28 Therefore take the talent from him, and give it to him who has ten talents. 29 For to everyone who has, more will be given, and he will have abundance; but from him who does not have, even what he has will be taken away.

STUDY GUIDE

Share in Prayer

See the Godly Perspective

John Keynes thought he had a new idea: borrow your way out of debt. He taught that governments could step in and solve national economic problems by offsetting demand – thus requiring excessive debt, inflation, and loss of personal liberty. Throughout this session, notice that God addressed this idea long ago and made it quite clear that debt produces slavery, not freedom or success.

Search For Truth

In recent years the U.S. government has "bailed out" failing businesses, claiming that they were just too big to let them fail. It may have sounded charitable to give money to companies that had poorly managed their assets and budgets with the intention of saving jobs, but where did that money come from? Governments do not have money of their own. Government must obtain money from: 1) taxing producers, 2) inflating the currency, or 3) borrowing from other nations. A "bail out" is not producing a solution. It is merely rearranging and increasing debt, which is not only harmful, but unscriptural. In all three of these options, one group is helped while another is severely hurt, whether it be from increasing prices for everyone because of inflation, higher taxes for future generations from borrowing, or lost jobs caused by downsizing when producers are forced to deal with increased taxation.

In this episode we'll see that the intent of Keynesian economics was not to glorify God, but to glorify man and destroy Biblical economics. Watch as the two worldviews stand in stark contrast: one supporting greed by giving man whatever he wants whenever he wants it, and the other supporting contentment by providing for the needy, working hard, and glorifying God through honest labor and profit.

Watch as followers of John Keynes seek to dig their way out of the hole of debt by borrowing, taxing producers, and inflating currency (printing more money out of thin air). All three actually damage the economy. Notice that, contrary to this worldly system, God gave us a better plan. *Godonomics* allows us to use material things like money to help ourselves and our fellow man. Observe throughout this session that according to the Bible, debt is not the solution – it is the problem!

Start the DVD Session and Specify the Worksheet Answers

(33 minutes)

GODONOMIC$

WORKSHEET

Both sides of the U.S. political structure follow the economic ideas of

_____ _____ .
    (1)   (2)

John Keynes' wisdom on money is almost the direct _____ of
                                                              (3)
what God teaches about money.

Keynesian Economic$ vs. Capitalistic Economic$

"The best way to destroy the capitalist system is to debauch the currency. By a continuing process of inflation, governments can confiscate, secretly and unobserved, an important part of the wealth of their citizens. There is no subtler, no surer means of overturning the existing basis of society than to debauch the currency. The process engages all the hidden forces of economic law on the side of destruction, and does it in a manner which not one man in a million is able to diagnose."

— *John Keynes*

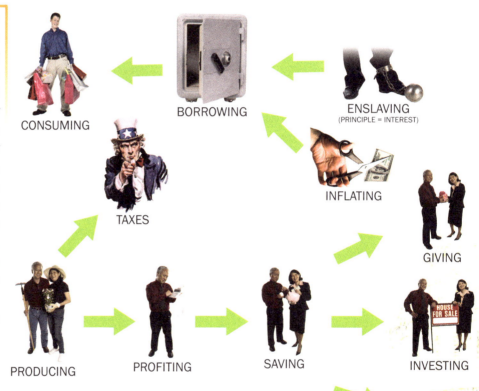

CONSUMING · BORROWING · ENSLAVING (PRINCIPLE = INTEREST) · TAXES · INFLATING · GIVING · PRODUCING · PROFITING · SAVING · INVESTING · SPENDING

Following John Keynes' economic ideas leads to

_____ .
    (4)

Godonomics is based upon _____ .
                                  (5)

Keynesian Economics is based upon _____ .
                                          (6)

www.usdebtclock.org

US NATIONAL DEBT	DEBT PER CITIZEN	DEBT PER TAXPAYER
$ 13,287,954,513,887	$42,876	$119,942

"Compound interest is one of the most powerful forces in the universe."

— *Albert Einstein*

John Keynes wanted to destroy _____ .
                                       (7)

WORKSHEET

2

SESSION

Remember: *Godonomics* is about God wanting us to experience Three Components: Liberty, Prosperity, and _____.
(8)

Godonomics Slogan #1:

WE SPEND OUR WAY TO SLAVERY, NOT PROSPERITY!

Borrowing leads to _____.
(9)

John Keynes "If you owe your bank manager a thousand pounds, you are at his mercy. If you owe him a million pounds, he is at your mercy."

Romans 13:8
    Owe no one anything except to love one another, for he who loves another has fulfilled the law.

Proverbs 22:7
    The borrower is servant to the lender.

The principles of *Godonomics* applies to_____as well as families and individuals.
(10)

God wants us to be_____.
(11)

"Reason does not suffer us to admit that all usury is to be condemned without exception… that is only as to the poor. If we have to do with the rich, that usury is freely permitted…. Usury is not now unlawful. Let each one, then, place himself before God's judgment-seat, and not do to his neighbor what he would not have done to himself."

— John Calvin

Godonomics Slogan #2: ACT YOUR OWN WAGE!

In order to act our own wage, Christians must look:
    1. _____ (12)
Luke 12:34
    Where your treasure is, there your heart will be also.
    2. _____ (13)
Proverbs 13:7
    There are some who pretend to be rich, yet have nothing. There are some who pretend to be poor, yet have great wealth.
    3. _____ (14)
Matthew 25: 15, 16, 20
    [15]And to one he gave five talents, to another two, and to another one, to each according to his own ability; and immediately he went on a journey. [16]Then he who had received the five talents went and traded with them, and made another five talents. [20]So he who had received five talents came and brought five other talents, saying, "Lord, you delivered to me five talents; look, I have gained five more talents besides them."

WORKSHEET

SESSION 2

Howard Dayton in his book *Your Money Counts* gives three principles to think about before borrowing. He said to consider whether:

- The item purchased is an asset with potential to appreciate or _____ (15) _____ (16).
- The value of the item _____ (17) or _____ (18) the amount owed against it.
- The debt is so large that repayment _____ (19) on the budget.

The material world is not bad; money can be used for

_____. (20)

I Timothy 6:10
    For the love of money is the root of all evil: which while some coveted after, they have erred from the faith, and pierced themselves through with many sorrows.

Deuteronomy 28:12,43,44
    [12]The Lord will open to you His good treasure... You shall lend to many nations, but <u>you shall not borrow</u>... [43]The alien who is among you shall rise <u>higher and higher</u> above you, and you <u>shall come down lower and lower</u>. [44]He shall lend to you, but you shall not lend to him; he shall be the head, and you shall be the tail.

Biblical capitalism implements the _____ (21) _____ (22) in economy. *"Do unto others as ye would have them do unto you."*

The reformer _____ (23) _____ (24) produced a new way of thinking regarding money and interest; thus producing a wave of prosperity.

Practicing *Godonomics* gives _____. (25)

We owe God a spiritual debt we cannot _____ (26); so Jesus _____ (27) it for us.

1 John 2:2
    And he is the propitiation for our sins: and not for ours only, but also for the sins of the whole world.

WORKSHEET SCORE KEY

1) John

2) Keynes

3) opposite

4) socialism

5) producing

6) consuming

7) capitalism

8) Generosity

9) slavery

10) nations

11) free

12) Inward

13) Backward

14) Forward

15) produce

16) income

17) equals

18) exceeds

19) puts undue strain

20) good

21) Golden

22) Rule

23) John

24) Calvin

25) contentment

26) pay

27) paid

Settle the Discussion Questions

1. Historically, democrats tax and spend, Republicans borrow and spend, and both parties inflate and spend. How might the Biblical principles of free enterprise, budgeting, and limited spending provide a solution to budget deficits and a lagging economy? _____

   _____

   _____

   _____

   _____

   _____

   _____

   _____

2. Keynes said, "If you owe your bank manager a thousand pounds, you are at his mercy. If you owe him a million pounds, he is at your mercy." If a person believes this quote by Keynes, how might that person address his own debt? _____

   _____

   _____

3. How is the focus of *Godonomics* different from that of Keynesian economics? _____

   _____

   _____

   _____

   _____

Study the Summary Statements

In America, both sides of the political establishment are Keynesians, and so the "debate" often excludes actual solutions. The options discussed are only matters of how much regulation or debt is necessary, which way we should spend more than we have, and how we can build government revenue via taxation, borrowing, or inflation. *Godonomics* teaches us to stop spending and to stop borrowing.

Both governments and individuals should stop living outside of their means. The solution to our debt problems is not to get another credit card, but to stop the spending. This is true at any level of the economy. Keynesian wisdom promotes our needs and wants as a top priority, even if we can't afford them. This yields an "entitlement mentality" of believing we deserve what we can't afford. However, God tells us to be content with the things we have – and only God can offer true and lasting contentment. Rather than practicing Keynesian Economics and being enslaved to debt and our own selfish desires, we have the opportunity to practice *Godonomics* and experience true economic and spiritual freedom through Jesus Christ.

Show Support

Write out I Timothy 6:6.

1 Timothy 6:6   "But Godliness with contentment is great gain."

List at least one way you want to see our nation practice *Godonomics* contentment rather than Keynesian economics greed in our national economy. _____

_____

_____

_____

List at least one way you want to practice *Godonomics* contentment rather than Keynesian economics greed in your personal life.

_____

_____

_____

Scripture to Savor

Proverbs 22:7
        The rich rules over the poor, and the **borrower is servant to the lender**.

"So . . . What *Would* God Say to John Keynes?"

STOP OVERSPENDING AND STOP BORROWING!
~ GOD

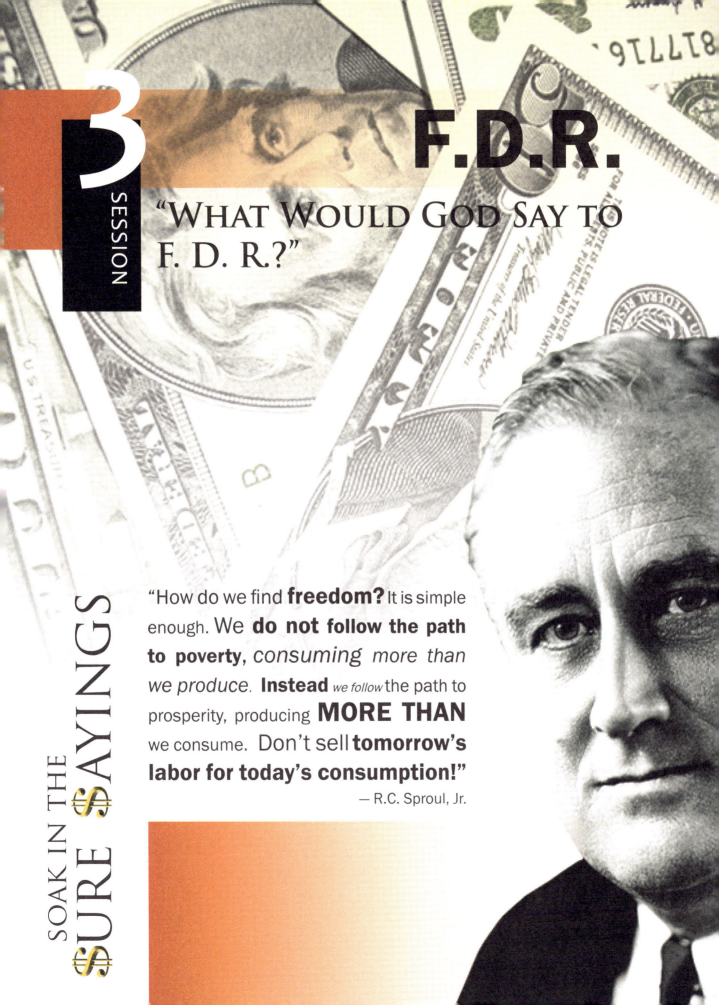

3
SESSION

F.D.R.

"WHAT WOULD GOD SAY TO F. D. R.?"

SOAK IN THE
$URE $AYINGS

"How do we find **freedom?** It is simple enough. We **do not follow the path to poverty,** *consuming* *more than we produce.* **Instead** *we follow* the path to prosperity, producing **MORE THAN** we consume. Don't sell **tomorrow's labor for today's consumption!"**

— R.C. Sproul, Jr.

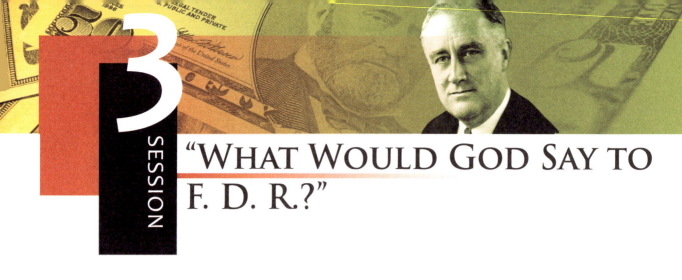

SESSION 3

"WHAT WOULD GOD SAY TO F. D. R.?"

INTRODUCTION

In this third session of *Godonomics*, "What Would God Say to F.D.R.?" we'll discuss two more paramount principles from *Godonomics*: Number One — "Don't exchange borrowing for budgeting!" and Number Two — "Don't exchange Liberty for Security!" In our exposure and education about the Great Depression, most of us were taught that Franklin Delano Roosevelt's "New Deal" rescued our national economy. By taking a closer look at F.D.R.'s economic politics through the eyeglass of Godonomic principles, we'll discover that the Great Depression was caused by his overspending, overinflating, and overborrowing. As we continue to use F.D.R.'s template in the current economic crisis, the results will be the same unless we understand and apply another Godonomic principle for dealing with a financial crisis — simply spend less than we make. Responsible spending must be practiced by ourselves. We in turn, must teach our children these truths for *Godonomics* can revolutionize our national economics!

James 4:13-14
*   [13] Come now, you who say, "Today or tomorrow we will go to such and such a city, spend a year there, buy and sell, and make a profit"; [14] whereas you do not know what will happen tomorrow. For what is your life? It is even a vapor that appears for a little time and then vanishes away.*

STUDY GUIDE

Share in Prayer

See the Godly Perspective

When we buy things on credit, we are spending tomorrow's money today. Would God be pleased with this lack of responsibility? Ephesians teaches that we should redeem the time, because the days are evil, and Proverbs instructs us that we should leave an inheritance for our children's children. Debt robs us of this opportunity. When we buy things today with money we don't have, we are pushing back the consequences of our actions until another day. God's way, however, is **to produce** in order to spend, **not to borrow** in order to spend.

Search For Truth

Keep an eye out for what God would say to F. D. R. throughout this episode: Don't spend tomorrow's money today. It's that simple. Greed often tricks our minds into believing we must have something — even at the expense of increasing debt. Notice that this seems to be the ongoing problem with both sides of the political aisle in America, and that a third way – God's way – needs to be followed.

Chad says in this session: "It's **unwise** to spend all of **today's** money today. It's **foolish** to spend all of **tomorrow's** money today, but it's **immoral** to spend **someone else's** money today." Listen carefully to the admonition of Proverbs 15:22 regarding inheritance and reflect on the stark contrast to what was passed down to future generations by F.D.R.

Finally, listen for the only path to true and lasting prosperity. Looking to the government as our security and solution leaves us unable to experience the true liberty and security God has for His followers!

Start the DVD Session and Specify the Worksheet Answers

(33 minutes)

SESSION 3

WORKSHEET

Both sides of the American political structure practice two unscriptural things:_____ _____ and _____.
(1) (2) (3)

Exchange #1:
DON'T EXCHANGE _____ FOR _____
(4) (5)

Don't Spend _____ Money _____!
(6) (7)
Proverbs 21:20

Former U.S. Government Chief Auditor *David Walker For more information, go to www.iousathemovie.com (This is a half hour movie clip put together by David Walker, former comptroller of the United States, showing just how perilous America's situation is.)*

There is desirable treasure, and oil in the dwelling of the wise, but a foolish man squanders it.
(8) (9)

The _____ man _____ all of today's money today and sometimes even consumes some of tomorrow's money today!
(10) (11)

The _____ man _____ some of today's profits so he can invest in tomorrow's ventures, jobs, and expansions.

Applying this principle of *Godonomics* allows the wise man to:
- Be radically generous.
- Invest in future economic endeavors with available capital.
- Spend wisely.

Proverbs 15:22
A good man leaves an _____ to his children's children.
(12)

Spending tomorrow's money today is "_____ _____."
(13) (14)

We don't break _____ _____, we discover them.
(15) (16)

DOW JONES INDUSTRIAL AVERAGE
10/01/1928 THRU 12/31/1954

WEEKLY CHANGE PRICE

25 YEARS

Hoover increases debt spending by 47% in four years.

450 400 350 300 250 200 150 100 50 0

1928 1930 1932 1934 1936 1938 1940 1942 1944 1946 1948 1952 1954

DOW JONES INDUSTRIAL AVERAGE
10/01/1928 THRU 12/31/1954

WEEKLY CHANGE PRICE

25 YEARS

FDR'S Presidency (1933-45)

First New Deal

Second New Deal

450 400 350 300 250 200 150 100 50 0

1928 1930 1932 1934 1936 1938 1940 1942 1944 1946 1948 1952 1954

WORKSHEET

What caused the Great Depression? Deficit _____
(17)

What brought us out of the Great Depression? _____
(18)

An infusion of borrowed money into an economy – personal or national – can appear to be prosperity at first, when in fact, it is only a "sugar high," that will eventually crash.
Luke 12:15
And He said to them, "Take heed and beware of covetousness, for one's life does not consist in the abundance of the things he possesses."

Budgeting is actually writing down your economic _____.
Ecclesiastes 11:2   (19)
"Give a serving to seven, and also to eight, for you do not know what evil will be on the earth."
This passage teaches that because we live in an evil world, we should prepare for difficult times by _____ our savings.
(20)

Don't _____ upon unknown income and economic gain.
(21)

Exchange #2:
DON'T EXCHANGE _____ FOR _____
(22)   (23)

Governments have no _____.
(24)

1 Samuel 8:4-9 warns that whatever a king offers in _____, he will take away from your _____.
(25)
(26)
(27)

I Samuel 8:19 says, "Nevertheless the people _____ the voice of Samuel; and they said, Nay; but we will have a king over us;"

When Israel chose a king, the king _____ them, hurting their ability to produce, profit, save, and give. (28)

Throughout history, Christ followers have wanted _____
(29)
_____.
(30)

Diversified power in the US Constitution was employed because when total power is given to any sinful man, it results in _____ (31) from the _____ for the selfish consumption of the rulers.
(32)

Surrendering to King _____ and His wisdom yields true security and liberty.
(33)

For further Study: *If you are interested in more information about Hoover's deficit spending, and the depression within the depression caused by the policies of FDR, go to www. cato.org The Cato Institute is a libertarian think tank of scholars that have done mountains of research on the Great Depression, how FDR's policies prolonged the Great Depression, and how free market policies actually solved the Great Depression of 1920.*

Habakkuk 2:2
Write the vision; and make it plain on tablets, that he may run who reads it.

Ephesians 5:16
Redeeming the time, because the days are evil."

Galatians 5:13
For you, brethren, have been called to liberty; only do not use liberty as an opportunity for the flesh, but through love serve one another.

3
SESSION

WORKSHEET SCORE KEY

1) over

2) spending

3) borrowing

4) borrowing

5) budgeting

6) Tomorrow's

7) Today

8) foolish

9) consumes

10) wise

11) saves

12) inheritance

13) Deficit

14) Spending

15) God's

16) Laws

17) Spending

18) Producing

19) vision

20) diversifying

21) presume

22) Liberty

23) Security

24) money

25) security

26) liberty

27) refused to obey

28) taxed

29) limited

30) government

31) taking

31) producers

32) Jesus

Settle the Discussion Questions

1. Did your education and upbringing teach you that the practices and policies of FDR's New Deal helped our economy? What are the ramifications for today if this is not true, and the New Deal policies actually hurt the economy? _____

   _____

   _____

   _____

   _____

2. What is at the root of consumer economics? What drives us to make purchases with money we do not have? How is this different from the driving force of *Godonomics*? _____

   _____

   _____

   _____

   _____

3. How was King Saul's rule different from God's rule over Israel? What were the effects of installing a king over Israel?

   _____

   _____

   _____

   _____

   _____

Study the Summary Statements

The question facing the Christian is often which king he will choose. In whom will he place his trust? We often place our trust in man-made governments to solve our problems and provide security. We ignore God's warning that strong and intrusive governments take away the liberty that is so vital to *Godonomics*. By trading liberty for security, we lose the freedom to manage our finances according to God's laws. Excessive man-made governments consume our wealth and diminish our capability to invest and generously give to others. The moment we embrace man's devices is the moment we become less free and less prosperous. Limited government fosters a prosperous economy and frees us to manage our resources as we are led by God.

Placing our faith in the King who sacrificed Himself for us is the first step in grasping the principles of *Godonomics*. By trusting the economic wisdom God gives us in Scripture, we can avoid being enslaved to debt and enjoy the freedom and prosperity King Jesus offers.

"I am in favor of cutting taxes under any circumstances and for any excuse, for any reason, whenever it's possible. The reason I am is because I believe the big problem is not taxes, the big problem is spending."

– Milton Friedman, American economist

Show Support

In 1 Samuel 8:6-20 God uses Samuel to forewarn the people about the problems with looking to an earthly king and expanding the role of government. Circle how many times the phrases "his" and "yours" are used. Then underline the number of times Samuel warns that the "king will take."

1 Samuel 8:6-20

6 But the thing displeased Samuel when they said, "Give us a king to judge us." So Samuel prayed to the LORD. 7And the LORD said to Samuel, "Heed the voice of the people in all that they say to you; for they have not rejected you, but they have rejected Me, that I should not reign over them. 8According to all the works which they have done since the day that I brought them up out of Egypt, even to this day--with which they have forsaken Me and served other gods--so they are doing to you also. 9Now therefore, heed their voice. However, you shall solemnly forewarn them, and show them the behavior of the king who will reign over them. 10 So Samuel told all the words of the LORD to the people who asked him for a king. 11 And he said, "This will be the behavior of the king who will reign over you: He will take your sons and appoint them for his own chariots and to be his horsemen, and some will run before his chariots. 12 He will appoint captains over his thousands and captains over his fifties, will set some to plow his ground and reap his harvest, and some to make his weapons of war and equipment for his chariots. 13 He will take your daughters [to be] perfumers, cooks, and bakers. 14 And he will take the best of your fields, your vineyards, and your olive groves, and give them to his servants. 15 He will take a tenth of your grain and your vintage, and give it to his officers and servants. 16 And he will take your male servants, your female servants, your finest young men, and your donkeys, and put them to his work. 17 He will take a tenth of your sheep. And you will be his servants. 18 And you will cry out in that day because of your king whom you have chosen for yourselves, and the LORD will not hear you in that day." 19 Nevertheless the people refused to obey the voice of Samuel; and they said, "No, but we will have a king over us, 20that we also may be like all the nations, and that our king may judge us and go out before us and fight our battles."

ADDITIONAL READING:

Biblical Economics
By R.C. Sproul Jr.

The Forgotten Man
By Shlaes Amity

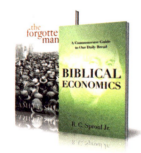

$Scripture to $avor

Proverbs 13:22

A good man leaves **an inheritance** to his children's children, But the wealth of the sinner is stored up for the righteous.

Deuteronomy 28:44

He shall lend to you, but **you shall not lend** to him; he shall be the head, and you shall be the tail.

"So . . . What *Would* God Say to FDR?"

STOP SPENDING TOMORROW'S MONEY TODAY!
~ GOD

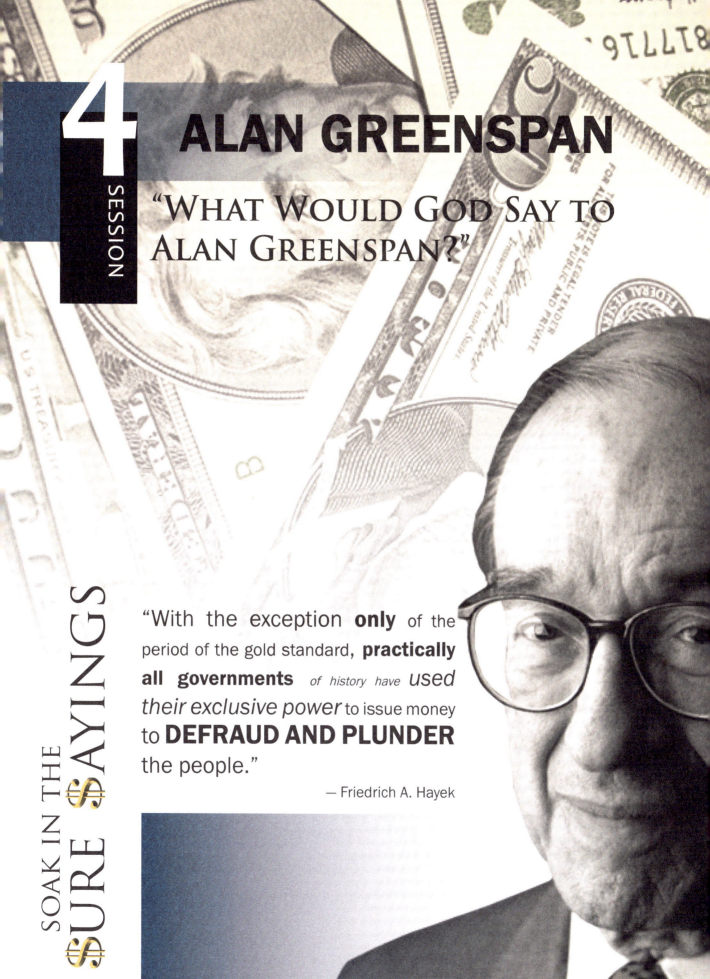

ALAN GREENSPAN

"What Would God Say to Alan Greenspan?"

"With the exception **only** of the period of the gold standard, **practically all governments** *of history have* used *their exclusive power* to issue money to **DEFRAUD AND PLUNDER** the people."

— Friedrich A. Hayek

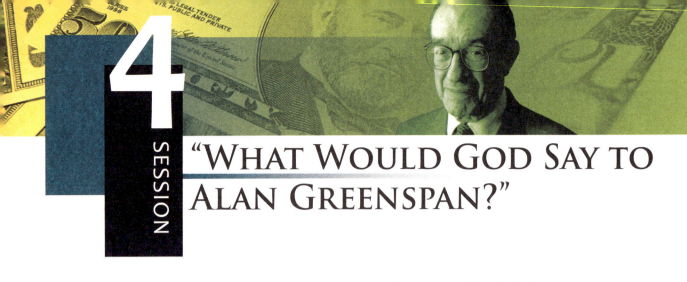

"WHAT WOULD GOD SAY TO ALAN GREENSPAN?"

INTRODUCTION

In our fourth session, "What Would God Say to Alan Greenspan?" we'll investigate three illusions, the Illusion of Value, the Illusion of Abundance, and the Illusion of Generosity. We'll gain an understanding of the true meaning of inflation, the cause of rising prices, the cause of home devaluation, and the cause of our economic crash.

If someone came into your house and over time slowly stole more than half of your possessions, would you want to know who did it and how they did it? Do you wonder what caused your house to drop in price 20, 30, 40, or even 50%? This session demonstrates how our dollars have been robbed of their buying power by 90% over the past 100 years.

Do you consider yourself a generous or a greedy person? Plunge into this session to evaluate what type of standard we are using for that determination.

Do you ever wonder if God really cares about money and the economy? Let's gain insight from God's instructions in the book of Proverbs on the importance He places on sound money rather than dishonest scales!

Luke 12:16-21

¹⁶Then He spoke a parable to them, saying: "The ground of a certain rich man yielded plentifully. ¹⁷And he thought within himself, saying, 'What shall I do, since I have no room to store my crops?' ¹⁸So he said, 'I will do this: I will pull down my barns and build greater, and there I will store all my crops and my goods.'" ¹⁹And I will say to my soul, "Soul, you have many goods laid up for many years; take your ease; eat, drink, and be merry."' ²⁰But God said to him, 'Fool! This night your soul will be required of you; then whose will those things be which you have provided?' ²¹"So is he who lays up treasure <u>for himself,</u> and is <u>not rich toward God</u>."

STUDY GUIDE

Share in Prayer

See the Godly Perspective

Think about it – how stable can an economy truly be, if the stability of the currency is not based on an asset such as gold or oil, but is rather based on the promise of good financial management? Most paper currencies are based solely on that promise alone. Our government has so poorly managed our money with overspending and excessive borrowing that we are up to 110 trillion dollars in debt. Would the God who always backs up His promises with real wealth be pleased with a system of empty promises? Can anyone truly be wealthy and secure in their property and resources when it is all based on paper promises? God demands sound money, just weights, and fair scales!

Search For Truth

We now come to the point in this series where a primary mechanism of consumer economics is revealed. Watch for three financial illusions by which humans are prone to be duped in their finances. Glean a new understanding of the role the Federal Reserve System plays in our economy when they print fiat money – paper currency backed by nothing of any real value. Notice how the Federal Reserve System, a privately-owned banking institution, creates the illusion of a booming economy by lowering interest rates resulting in devalued, but abundant cash. This false economy would not be such a powerful, enslaving mechanism were it not for our tendency towards a problem with which every human being struggles. With *Godonomics*, learn how to unmask these three illusions impressed upon us by ourselves, as well as by others!

Start the DVD Session and Specify the Worksheet Answers

(32 minutes)

WORKSHEET

SESSION 4

Illusion #1: THE ILLUSION OF_____
(1)

Micah 6:11 Shall I acquit a man with dishonest scales, with a bag of <u>false weights</u>?

The illusion of value comes from _____scales.
(2)

The value of money used to be tied to a _____. In America, the commodity was gold.
(3)

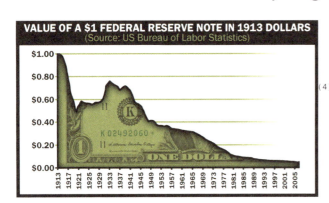

When President Woodrow Wilson wanted to print more money without getting more gold, he exchanged the commodity of gold for a
(4)
_____ to make good economic decisions.
(5)   (6)

The _____ _____ steals our money without the public ever knowing it, or ever realizing the scales have been changed.

Proverbs 11:1
<u>Dishonest scales are an abomination</u> to the LORD, but a just weight is His delight.

Deut 25:15
If you <u>weigh and measure things honestly</u>, the LORD your God will let you enjoy a long life in the land he is giving you.

For Further Study: _Go to the government website at the Bureau of Labor Statistics and check it out for yourself. If you put in 100 dollars of 1913 bills, what could they be worth today? Or said differently, what could they buy today? The calculator will tell you how much buying power has been stolen through inflation, the devaluing of the dollar._ _http://www.bls.gov/data/inflation_calculator.htm_

God cares about _____.
(7)

According to Keynesian Economics, "prices going up" is _____.
(8)
Austrian economists note that rising prices is not inflation – inflation_____in higher prices.
(9)

The Federal Reserve printed more money and therefore _____ the dollar.
(10)

Proverbs 14:31
He who <u>oppresses the poor</u> reproaches his Maker, but he who honors Him has <u>mercy on the needy</u>.

Proverbs 11:14
"Where no counsel is, the people fall: but in the **multitude of counselors** there is safety."

WORKSHEET

Illusion #2: THE ILLUSION OF _____
(11)

Luke 12:15

     And he said unto them, Take heed, and beware of covetousness: for a man's life consisteth not in the abundance of the things which he possesseth.

The Faces of Greed include:

- _____ (12)
- _____ (13)
- _____ (14)
- _____ (15)
- _____ (16)

> *Luke 21:1-4*
>
>   *¹And He looked up and saw the rich putting their gifts into the treasury, ²and He saw also a certain poor widow putting in two mites. ³So He said, "Truly I say to you that this poor widow has put in more than all; ⁴for all these <u>out of their abundance</u> have put in offerings for God, but <u>she out of her poverty</u> put in all the livelihood that she had."*

Everybody struggles with greed. The only wise thing to do is assume that you too struggle with _____.
(17)

The reasons for greed often seem smart or legitimate, but the problem is being rich toward _____, not toward _____.
(18) (19)

Illusion #3: THE ILLUSION OF _____
(20)

The illusion of generosity means we measure or define generosity by our own _____ of what we are doing.
(21)

The average Christ follower gives away less than ____% of their income.
(22)

God speaks of giving in terms of _____, _____, and _____ becoming more generous.
(23) (24)
(25)

Godonomics is not about giving out of **your abundance**, but rather about
(26) _____ your life in such a way to produce, profit, and save so that you can be _____ _____ to others.
(27) (28)

If we struggle with generosity, we need to look deeper into Jesus' _____ for us.
(29)

2 Corinthians 8:9

     For ye know the grace of our Lord Jesus Christ, that, <u>though he was rich</u>, yet for your sakes he <u>became poor</u>, that ye through his poverty might be rich.

ADDITIONAL READING:

Fields of Gold

Andy Stanley

WORKSHEET SCORE KEY

1) Value

2) dishonest

3) commodity

4) promise

5) Federal

6) Reserve

7) money

8) inflation

9) results

10) devalued

11) Abundance

12) Hoarding

13) Overspending

14) Entitlement

15) Coveting

16) Discount

17) greed

18) yourself

19) God

20) Generosity

21) standard

22) 2

23) percentages

24) priorities

25) progressively

26) organizing

27) lavishly

28) generous

29) sacrifice

Settle the Discussion Questions

1. How does printing money we don't have to help the poor actually hurt the poor? _____

_____

_____

_____

_____

2. Why is "sound money," money that is tied to a commodity like gold, a fair and just economic principle for everyone? _____

_____

_____

_____

_____

_____

3. What causes a housing bubble, and why does it fail to reflect real value? _____

_____

_____

_____

_____

_____

Study the Summary Statements

Jesus gave His very best for us, and so we should for Him. How do we do that? The Bible tells us helping others is like giving to Him. The driving force of *Godonomics* is spending, investing, and giving, not just for ourselves, but for others.

In a consumer-based economy manipulated by private banks like the Federal Reserve through which our wealth and financial security become unstable, generosity is more difficult for us. This is why God would tell Alan Greenspan and all other chairmen of the Federal Reserve to stop the presses! Stop devaluing our currency! Though we don't like to admit it, we are to blame too. We all deal with greed on some level.

Like the widow who gave her last two mites, we should give our best to others as unto the Lord. We can raise our children to give generously in spite of the errors of others, while also teaching them the Biblical way governments should approach economy. *Godonomics* reaches beyond governmental policies and personal budgeting capabilities. It reaches into the very heart and soul within us and teaches us the true spirit behind giving to the needs of others.

Show Support

Choose one of the verses discussed in this session that has made you rethink your finances and copy it below. List how you wish to apply this verse in your life.

Verse:

_____
_____
_____
_____
_____
_____

ADDITIONAL READING:

The Treasure Principle
Randy Alcorn

The Rise of Christianity (Traces the impact of Christianity and charity on the modern world)
Rodney Star

Application:

_____
_____
_____
_____
_____
_____
_____
_____
_____
_____
_____
_____
_____

Scripture to Savor

Proverbs 20:23

Diverse weights are an abomination to the LORD, and dishonest scales are not good.

Micah 6:10-11

[10]Are there yet the treasures of wickedness in the house of the wicked, and the short measure that is an abomination? [11]Shall I count pure those with the wicked scales, and with the bag of deceitful weights?

"So . . . What *Would* God say to Alan Greenspan?"

STOP THE PRESSES!
~ GOD

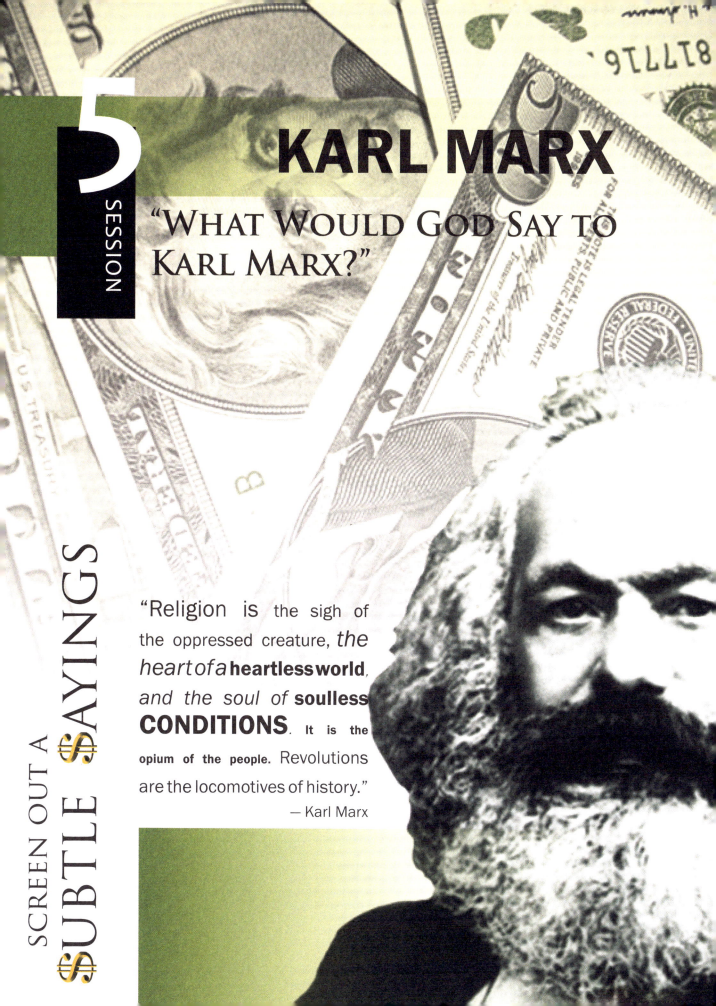

KARL MARX

"WHAT WOULD GOD SAY TO KARL MARX?"

SCREEN OUT A $UBTLE $AYINGS

"Religion is the sigh of the oppressed creature, *the heart of a* **heartless world**, *and the soul of* **soulless CONDITIONS**. It is the **opium of the people.** Revolutions are the locomotives of history."

— Karl Marx

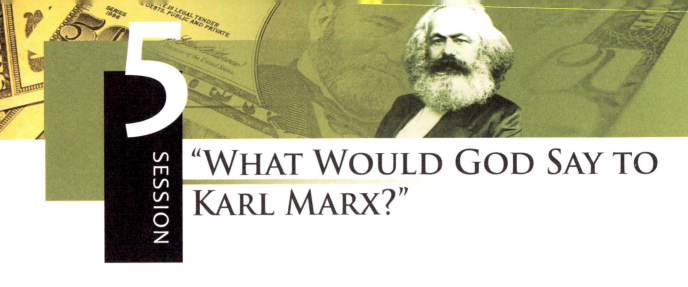

"WHAT WOULD GOD SAY TO KARL MARX?"

INTRODUCTION

In Session Five, "What Would God Say to Karl Marx?" we'll grabble with three important aspects of a national economy and how they impact our individual lives: The Scale, The Purchase, and The World View. God's principles of liberty, prosperity, and generosity are in complete contradiction to the teachings of Karl Marx and Communism. Looking through these two views, we'll find out how individuals, cities, and nations go from being prosperous to bankrupt!

How can we vote in such a way to keep prosperity a vital part of the future? This session will give us two tests that will allow us to size up a politician in either party and understand their basic view on economics in less than five minutes. We'll also be able to explain why and where the government is wasting our money and what we can do about it. Understanding first party, second party, and third party purchases will give us a more complete foundation for discerning why government purchases are always third party purchases that waste the tax payer's money.

Finally, we'll compare the American Revolution's proclamation for life, liberty and the pursuit of happiness with the French Revolution's cry for liberty, fraternity, and equality. We'll also review why the inalienable rights from our Creator were paramount in our constitution! Let's learn what God would say to Karl Marx!

STUDY GUIDE

5

Share in Prayer

See the Godly Perspective

God's greatest gift to us is freedom — freedom to choose — freedom to make mistakes. We can try to make ourselves prosperous, or trust the government to provide prosperity for us. The end result of both is the same: failure. True freedom and prosperity come from God as we practice His principles. Throughout Scripture, God has warned us that trusting in men, whether ourselves or governments, is not the answer. We should trust in God and His principles for freedom and prosperity. The Truth can then set us free.

Search For Truth

In Session Five, we'll study Three Aspects of a National Economy: The Scale, The Purchase, and The World View. Looking at these through the eyes of Karl Marx and the system that has come to bear his name, we see Karl Marx teaching that government can solve society's problems. No, Marx didn't put it quite that way, but if we watch closely, we will see how the principles of Socialism keep coming back to that basic assumption. Note how American history has exposed the fallacies of Socialistic promises.

Dare to compare Humanism with God's standards. Dare to look at the real differences between the American Revolution and the French Revolution. Discover the underlying secret to prosperity---both for an individual and for a nation.

Start the DVD Session and Specify the Worksheet Answers

(34 minutes)

WORKSHEET

5 SESSION

Karl Marx said he came to offer_____(1) In reality, Karl Marx offered a system in which he would have _____(2) _____(3). This stands in stark contrast to what we have been studying in *Godonomics*. God wants us to experience liberty, prosperity and generosity.

Four percent of the world has produced the most play wrights, the most inventions, and the biggest economic gains — _____(4)!

Fifty percent of the world lives on _____ dollars a day or less. (5)

Generosity can be traced back to the incredible _____ of America. (6)

Arkansas's Gross Domestic Product (GDP) is higher than the _____(7) largest nation in the world, Pakistan.

Louisiana's GDP is higher than the _____(8) largest nation in the world, Indosnesia.

The GDP of the entire nation of Russia is less than that of _____. (9)

In America, liberty has led to _____(10), which has led to generosity.

The _____(11) is inscribed with Leviticus 25:10.
    "And you shall consecrate the fiftieth year, and <u>proclaim liberty throughout all the land to all its inhabitants</u>. It shall be a Jubilee for you; and each of you shall return to his possession, and each of you shall return to his family."

The story of _____ has always been a part of Jesus' story. (12)

THREE ASPECTS OF GODONOMICS:
(13)

Aspect #1: _____
When someone takes away a percentage of your income, two things happen. You have:
    1. Less _____(14)
    2. Lower _____(15)
Someone who works all day long, but gets to take home none of their income is called a _____. (16)

WORKSHEET

We can evaluate the trajectory of a world leader by looking to see if he is moving the taxation scale of a nation toward more _____ (17) or more slavery.

The economy of every nation throughout history has demonstrated that the greater the freedom, the greater the_____, and the greater the government, the greater the _____. (18)
(19)
(20)

Under _____, tax dollars are funneled through an inefficient and often corrupt organization, and are not efficiently spent.

(21)

At one point, Detroit, Michigan, was the _____ city in America. Due to heavy taxation, out of the 26 largest cities in America, it is now the poorest.

A case study of North Korea and South Korea clearly demonstrates how The Scale works. In North Korea, 2.5 million people starve each year. In South Korea, her economy boasts the _____ (22) largest GDP in the world.

Government doesn't produce; it _____, enslaving us along the way.
(23)

Taxation Scale:
Percent the Producer Keeps

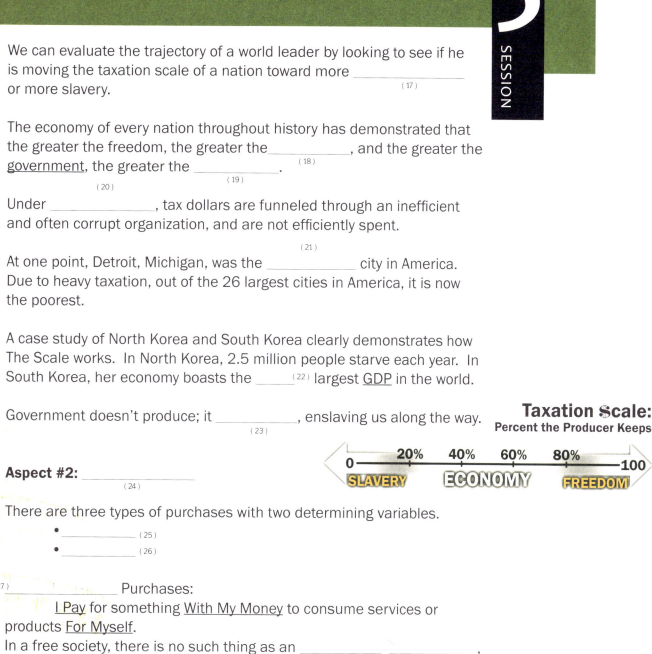

Aspect #2: _____
(24)

There are three types of purchases with two determining variables.

- _____ (25)
- _____ (26)

(27) _____ Purchases:
   I Pay for something With My Money to consume services or products For Myself.
In a free society, there is no such thing as an _____ _____, as long as the consumer is free to choose.
(28)   (29)

(30) _____ Purchases:
   I Pay for something With Someone Else's Money to consume services or products For Myself.
Or
   I Pay for something With My Money for services or products For Someone Else.

(31) _____ Purchases

    <u>I Pay</u> for something <u>With Someone Else's Money</u> for services or products <u>For Someone Else.</u>

All government purchases are _____ purchases.
                      (32)

Communist and Socialist countries build walls in order to keep their people in, so that the people might "_____!"
                                (33)

That's why President Reagan said, "_____ _____ that wall!"
                            (34)   (35)

Mark 8:35

    For whoever desires to save his life will lose it, but whoever loses his life for My sake and the gospel's will save it.

James 2:8

    If you really fulfill the royal law according to the Scripture, "You shall love your neighbor as yourself," you do well;

The more you _____ others, the more you receive!
              (36)

Aspect #3: _____
                 (37)

These two views of life impact how you view policies, responsibility, and problem-solving.

Humanism	God's Worldview
Man is good.	God is good, and man is in need of a Savior.
Man's environment is responsible for his behavior.	Man's environment is not responsible for his behavior; rather, the individual is responsible for his own behavior.
Man is the standard.	God is the standard.
Rights are granted by The Group.	Rights are granted by God.

The environment is not responsible for my problems: I, _____, am responsible.
                                         (38)

Declaration of Independence . . . "We hold these truths to be self-evident, that all men are created equal, that they are endowed by their Creator with certain unalienable Rights, that among these are _____, _____ and the pursuit of _____
         (39)   (40)   (41)
(Originally - _____). That to secure these rights, governments
             (42)
are instituted among men, deriving their just powers from the consent of the governed."

The theme of the French Revolution was Liberty, _____ (the
                                        (43)
Group, the Gang, the Soviet, the Union), and _____.
                                         (44)

Romans 3:23
For all have sinned, and come short of the glory of God;

Romans 5:8
But God commendeth his love toward us, in that, while we were yet sinners, Christ died for us.

Romans 6:23
For the wages of sin is death; but the gift of God is eternal life through Jesus Christ our Lord.

The _____(45) became the motivating symbol to persuade Frenchmen to become a part of the new group and the new equality, because their rights did not come from God. Their rights came from the Fraternity.

Ben Franklin's speech imploring his fellow countrymen to pray for wisdom while forming the constitution:

> "Mr. President, The small progress we have made after four or five weeks close attendance and continual reasonings with each other-our different sentiments on almost every question, several of the last producing as many noes as ays, is me thinks a melancholy proof of the imperfection of the Human Understanding. We indeed seem to feel our own want of political wisdom, since we have been running about in search of it. We have gone back to ancient history for models of Government, and examined the different forms of those Republics which having been formed with the seeds of their own dissolution, now no longer exist. And we have viewed Modern States all round Europe, but find none of their Constitutions suitable to our circumstances. In this situation of this Assembly, groping as it were in the dark to find political truth, and scarce able to distinguish it when presented to us, how has it happened, Sir, that we have not hitherto once thought of humbly applying to the Father of lights to illuminate our understandings? In the beginning of the Contest with Great Britain, when we were sensible of danger, we had daily prayer in this room for the Divine protection. Our prayers, Sir, were heard, and they were graciously answered. All of us who were engaged in the struggle must have observed frequent instances of a superintending providence in our favor. To that kind providence we owe this happy opportunity of consulting in peace on the means of establishing our future national felicity. And have we now forgotten that powerful friend? Or do we imagine that we no longer need his assistance? I have lived, Sir, a long time, and the longer I live, the more convincing proofs I see of this truth- that God governs in the affairs of men. And if a sparrow cannot fall to the ground without his notice, is it probable that an empire can rise without his aid? We have been assured, Sir, in the Sacred Writings, that "except the Lord build the house they labor in vain that build it." I firmly believe this; and I also believe that without his concurring aid, we shall succeed in this political building no better than the Builders of Babel. I therefore move that prayers imploring the assistance of Heaven and its blessing on our deliberation be held in this assembly every morning before we proceed to business."

The First Continental Congress then took three days for _____(46), _____(47), and _____(48) before coming back together as a group. Six weeks later, they had penned the Constitution of the United States of America.

Our inherent dignity and our inherent value does not come from the group. It comes from "creation ex deo"— created by the Heavenly Father.

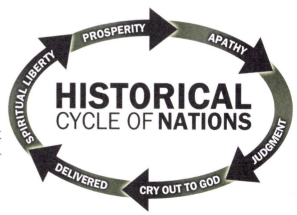

God _____(49), but we have not learned _____ both individually and as a nation! (50)

WORKSHEET SCORE KEY

5 SESSION

1) freedom

2) more

3) control

4) America

5) two

6) liberty

7) sixth

8) fourth

9) New Jersey

10) Prosperity

11) Liberty Bell

12) freedom

13) The Scale

14) Choices

15) Standard of Living

16) slave

17) freedom

18) wealth

19) poverty

20) Socialism

21) richest

22) 10th

23) consumes

24) The Purchase

25) Price

26) Quality

27) First Party

28) unfair

29) price

30) Second Party

31) Third Party

32) Third Party

33) enjoy the benifits

34) Tear

35) down

36) bless

37) The World View

38) individually

39) Life

40) Liberty

41) Happiness

42) Property

43) Fraternity

44) Equality

45) guillotine

46) fasting

47) prayer

48) worship

49) made us free

50) how to live free

Settle the Discussion Questions

1. **Read Proverbs 24:3-4. How do the principles of price and quality affect purchasing and investing? How do they motivate us to be wise and frugal in our financial choices?**_____

   _____

   _____

   _____

   _____

   _____

2. **What is a First-Party Purchase, and how is it different from a Third Party Purchase?**_____

   _____

   _____

   _____

   _____

   _____

3. **Compare/contrast the three ideals of the French Revolution to the three enshrined in the American Declaration of Independence.**

   _____

   _____

   _____

   _____

   _____

   _____

   _____

   Finally, Americans changed the order of the ideals, carefully and purposefully putting life ahead of liberty and happiness. Only when a nation truly respects and protects the sanctity of life can it enjoy liberty and the pursuit of happiness.

Study the Summary Statements

It's all connected. Like a string of upset dominoes, the compromise of the individual on these issues will rock the nation to its very core. When men and families no longer humble themselves before God, seeking to

implement His ways in all aspects of their lives – including finances and principles of government – then the community is weakened. They elect mayors, councilmen, state representatives, and eventually congressmen, senators, and presidents who do not acknowledge God or the principles of *Godonomics*. The resulting departure from Scriptural principles of fairness, frugality, brotherly kindness, limited government, free enterprise, and sound money then leads the whole nation into poverty and slavery. Like the indicator on The Taxation Scale, a nation will either sway towards freedom and prosperity, or towards more government intervention, increased taxes, less individual responsibility, less freedom, and less wealth beginning with the actions of the individuals who make up the nation. As Scripture bears out, when men leave God's governance, they are delivered over to governmental oppression. When they return to God, the Lord gives them freedom, which naturally results in the blessings and prosperity of God.

Show Support

List one "upset domino" in the chain of your life which you will reset this week to move your family toward a more Godonomic perspective. Some ideas would include: Memorize a Scripture; Invest the time to educate another American on the benefits of Godonomic principles; Make a specific change in how you will make your first party, second party, or third party purchases. _____

_____

_____

_____

_____

Evaluate where your family is on the Historical Cycle of Nations. If you are already in the "Prosperous Cycle," list at least one action you will undertake this week in order to help protect your family from falling into the "Apathy Cycle." If you are not in the "Prosperous Cycle," list at least one action you will undertake this week in order to begin moving your family to that place of God's blessing. _____

_____

_____

_____

_____

_____

Scripture to Savor

Leviticus 25:10

>And you shall consecrate the fiftieth year, and **proclaim liberty throughout all the land to all its inhabitants**.

2 Corinthians 3:17

>Now the Lord is the Spirit; and where the **Spirit of the Lord is, there is liberty**.

"So . . . What *Would* God Say to Karl Marx?"

GET A BARBER AND STOP TAKING AWAY
PEOPLE'S FREEDOM!
~ GOD

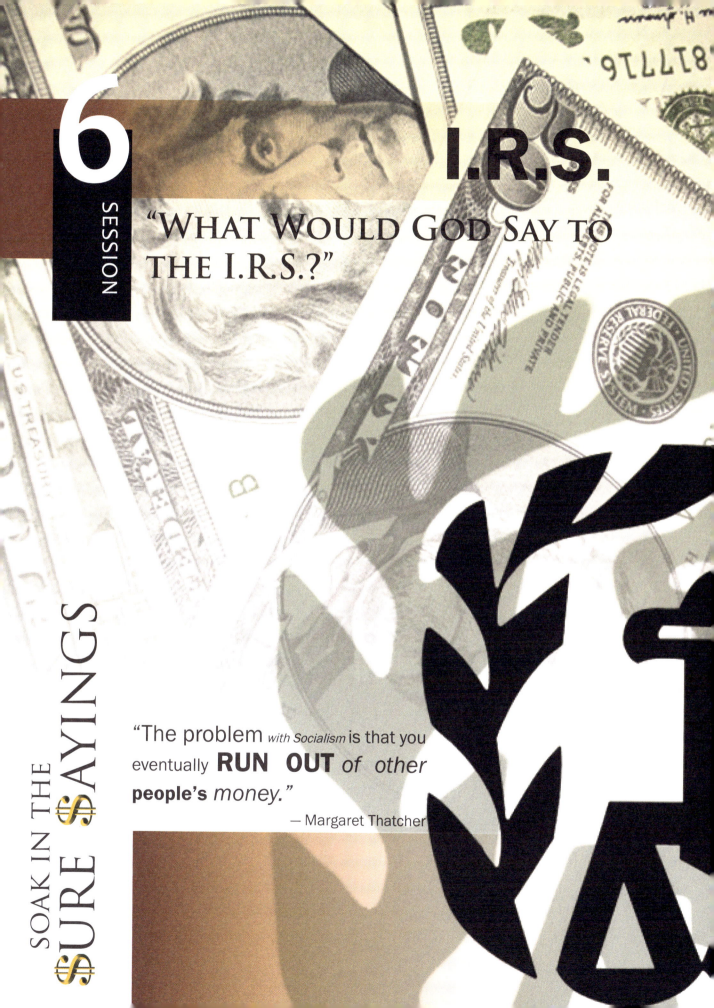

I.R.S.

"WHAT WOULD GOD SAY TO THE I.R.S.?"

6 SESSION

"The problem *with Socialism* is that you eventually **RUN OUT** of other people's *money*."

— Margaret Thatcher

SOAK IN THE SURE $AYINGS

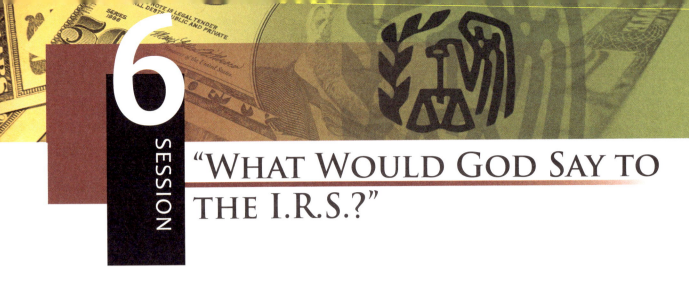

"WHAT WOULD GOD SAY TO THE I.R.S.?"

INTRODUCTION

In this sixth session of *Godonomics*, we'll enhance our understanding of <u>taxes</u>, of <u>coercion</u>, <u>and of the joy of individual generosity</u>. This section shows how God's Principles and common sense economic policies actually help the economy. We'll look at how both John F. Kennedy and Ronald Reagan's <u>lower tax rates</u> actually <u>increased tax revenue</u>. If you have wondered why companies today are shedding jobs and why states have to dramatically slash budgets, this chapter will help you grasp the relationship between taxation and employment.

We'll discover different types of giving and how they affect our hearts. What type of motivation for giving fills you with guilt, pride, or fear? Which type of giving fills you with peace, contentment, and true joy? God has a lot to say about submission — including paying taxes. However, God also warns us against pursuing excessive government that overtaxes its people and spends the revenue in wasteful ways. We will again visit the subjects of individualism versus collectivism, as clearly taught in the Scriptures, in relation to giving. Yes — *Godonomics* (what God has to say about economy and money) has a lot to say to the I.R.S.!

2 Corinthians 9:5-8

⁵Therefore I thought it <u>necessary to exhort</u> the brethren to go to you ahead of time, and prepare your generous gift beforehand, which you had previously promised, that it may be ready as <u>a matter of generosity</u> and not as a grudging obligation. ⁶But this I say: He who sows sparingly will also reap sparingly, and he who sows bountifully will also reap bountifully. ⁷So let <u>each one</u> give as he purposes in his heart, not grudgingly or of necessity; for God loves <u>a cheerful giver</u>. ⁸And God is able to make <u>all grace</u> abound toward you, that you, always having <u>all sufficiency in all things</u>, may have an abundance for every good work.

2 Corinthians 8:9

For you know the grace of our Lord Jesus Christ, that though He was rich, yet for your sakes <u>He became poor, that you through His poverty might become rich</u>.

STUDY GUIDE

6

Share in Prayer

See the Godly Perspective

If we were required to give a specific amount to a charity about which we cared absolutely nothing, would we give any more than the required amount? Probably not. This is a coercive approach, which forces us to give to causes and programs about which we don't care or necessarily approve. Begrudging giving is the result. This type of giving is not God's way.

But what if it we were required to give to a charity about which we were passionate, and we were given the opportunity to give of our own free will? We would probably give more abundantly because we would be giving out of a cheerful heart. That's *Godonomics*! God clearly instructs us to give individually and to give cheerfully out of a grateful heart.

Search For Truth

To Give: To relinquish; To yield; To proffer to another; To deliver; To make gifts or donations; Not keeping for oneself. Notice in this session the three primary ways giving can take place. Two of them involve coercion. Only one comes from the grace of God. *Godonomics* giving is motivated by thankfulness to God and a desire to pass along the grace bestowed on us. Government doesn't afford us this type of giving. Notice how neither major party in the American political system differs on this. While they may differ on <u>how</u> to coerce giving, neither abandon the concept of coercion itself.

Coercion is exercised by religious organizations also. In fact, this session reveals that many religious methods of coercion through fear and deceit are the same as the ones used by corrupt governments and politicians. Once again, listen for the stark contast of *Godonomics* verses coercion on the subject of giving!

Discover what the Laffer Curve is, and how it affects taxation and revenue. Can <u>lower taxes</u> actually <u>increase government revenue</u>? Follow history and see!

Start the DVD Session and Specify the Worksheet Answers

(28 minutes)

WORKSHEET

SESSION 6

Giving _____
(1)

2 Corinthians 9:5-8 (see page 60)

There are two types of coercion: _____ and _____ coercion.
(2) (3)

Coercive giving makes us more and more _____, rather than more and more cheerful.
(4)

Romans 13:7
"Render therefore to all their due: taxes to whom taxes are due."

Matthew 22:16
"Teacher, what do You think? Is it lawful to pay taxes to Caesar, or not?" "Render therefore to Caesar the things that are Caesar's, and to God the things that are God's."

(5)
Political _____

History of the IRS
1787   U.S. Constitution prohibited a "direct" federal tax
1862   "Revenue Tax" levied on incomes to finance the Union during the Civil War
1895   Supreme Court made Income Tax unconstitutional
1913   Income Tax of 1% levied on only the top 1% of producers (Invoked by President Woodrow Wilson)
1943   Withholding Tax from Paychecks invoked as an emergency effort to finance World War II

(6)
_____ does not align with the Democrats nor the Republicans, but rather is a whole new way of thinking about money and economics.

ADDITIONAL READING:

The Interesting History of Income Tax
William J. Federer

LAFFER CURVE

EQUILIBRIUM POINT

MAXIMUM REVENUE

REVENUE

Point A   Point B

NO REVENUE
0%   TAXES RATES   100%

(7)   (8)
"_____ rates of taxation will _____ economic activity and so raise the levels of personal and corporate income as to yield within a few years an _____ flow of revenues to the Federal Government."
(9)

Supply-side economics, as noted by Art Laffer, show that a _____
(10)
in _____ results in an _____ in tax _____.
(11)   (12)   (13)

WORKSHEET

President Franklin D. Roosevelt said that "the forgotten man" was the
_____ (14).

As illustrated in "The Forgotten Man" by Amity Shlaes, political coercion takes place when people are forced to give to those in need.

Amity Shlaes correctly demonstrates that the <u>real forgotten man</u> is the
_____. (15)

(16)

If someone is in need and we have extra, we should _____ to that person, but government should not _____ (17) / _____ (18) us to do so through taxation.

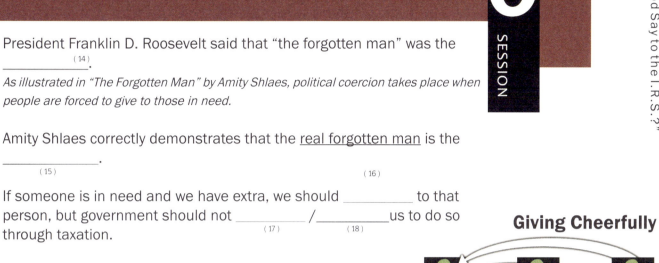

Giving Cheerfully

A — Person In Need   B — Has Extra   C — Has Extra

Religious _____ (19)
Guilt — Fear — Pride

These produce begrudging giving, attempt to manipulate God, and falsely assume that all God's blessings are materialistic.

Giving Begrudgingly

A — Person In Need   B — Government   C — The Producer

Giving _____ (20)

- Given without any attempt to make up for our sins
- Given with motivation of a grateful heart for God's grace
- Given with a confidence in God's promised provision for our needs
- Given as seeds to invest in God's work
- Given in response to what Christ gave for us, becoming poor that he might make us rich

When generosity is difficult for us, we do not need to try harder, but rather we must _____ (21) _____ (22) into the grace of Christ.

(23)

God gave us the means to _____ so we should _____
our profits to give and to invest that we might glorify Him. (24)

In our study of *Godonomics* we will have learned that **Socialism**
_____ (25) _____ (26), and that **Capitalism** doesn't eliminate
_____, but it does neutralize it. (27)

God's principles for economy will make you:
1. More _____ (28)   2. More _____ (29)   3. More _____ (30)

6 SESSION

WORKSHEET SCORE KEY

1) Begrudgingly

2) political

3) religious

4) bitter

5) Coercion

6) *Godonomics*

7) Lower

8) stimulate

9) increased

10) decrease

11) taxes

12) increase

13) revenue

14) poor

15) producer

16) give

17) coerce

18) force

19) Coercion

20) Cherrfully

21) look

22) deeper

23) produce

24) leverage

25) doesn't

26) work

27) greed

28) free

29) prosperous

30) generous

Settle the Discussion Questions

What was your favorite holiday growing up, or your favorite holiday now? Does it involve giving? What emotion does giving freely provide for you? When we give freely out of love, gratitude, or concern for others, we are obeying *Godonomics* giving principles. Obeying God's plan reaps many rewards---emotionally, spiritually, and financially.

1. **What are ways that religion can use coercion to bring about giving?**

   _____

   _____

   _____

2. **What are two ways lowering taxes might result in increased tax revenue?** _____

   _____

   _____

   _____

   _____

3. **Discuss F.D.R.'s Forgotten Man concept. How is coerced giving of this sort contrary to *Godonomics*? What is the only difference between the U.S. political parties as it pertains to this error?** _____

   _____

   _____

   _____

   _____

Study the Summary Statements

So, what can I do? You might be asking yourself this question now that you understand that government is not following God's laws of economics. *Godonomics* is not a magic formula for governments. *Godonomics* is a set of Biblical principles that every individual can live by, inspire others to live by, and encourage their leaders to live by. Think of the good God has done for us, and how He wants us to give out of our gratitude for these gifts. Rather than go along with the mentality of giving only what is required, embrace the Christian ideal of going the extra mile. Invest in others. Give to worthy ministries that are sharing God's gift with others.

Let's not get caught up in consumer economics, which puts consuming before producing, enslaving ourselves to debt because we "deserve" something we can't afford. Rather, let's manage our finances in accordance with the system of *Godonomics*: produce, then profit, then save; and then give, spend, and invest. The result? God's liberty, prosperity, and generosity!

$how $upport

What would God say to you?
Give of a cheerful heart, and it shall be given to you pressed down, shaken together, and running over.

Luke 6:38
Give and it shall be given to you: good measure, pressed down, shaken together, and running over will be put into your bosom. For with the same measure that you use, it will be measured back to you.

$cripture to $avor

2 Corinthians 9:7
So let each one give as he purposes in his heart, **not grudgingly** or of necessity; for God loves a **cheerful giver**.'

"So . . . What *Would* God Say to the I.R.S.?"

STOP COERCING PEOPLE TO GIVE!
~ GOD

YOU CAN'T GRANT PEOPLE TRUE
LIBERTY WITHOUT THE FOUNDATION
OF MY WORD.
~ GOD